Fuzzy ducklings peek over summer daisies.

Baby Farm Animals

by Merrill Windsor

BOOKS FOR YOUNG EXPLORERS
NATIONAL GEOGRAPHIC SOCIETY

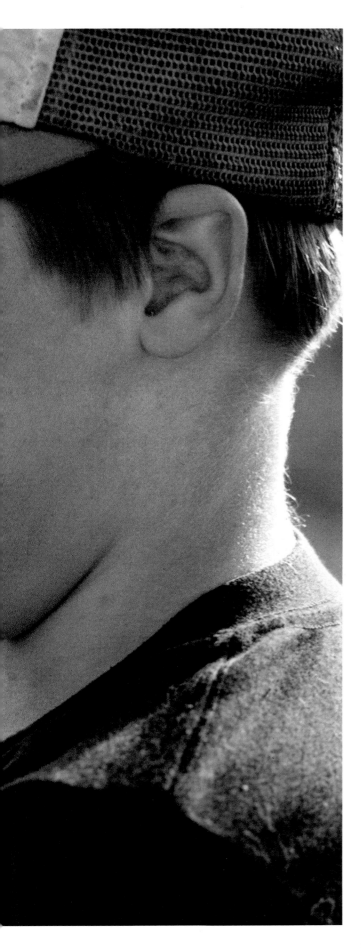

Nose to nose, Russell and
a piglet get to know each other.
Russell lives on a farm.
He likes the many animals there.

Best of all, he likes the small,
young ones. He feeds them and
cleans their pens. Baby farm
animals need a lot of care.

Have you ever been to a farm? This is a dairy farm. The long building where the cows are milked is the milking barn. In the round tower, called a silo, the farmer stores food for the cows.

A cow cleans her brand-new baby with her tongue. Not even one hour old, the calf is already trying to stand.

Soon the calf is on its feet. Its legs are not very steady, but it can walk beside its mother.

Dairy calves can be born at any time of year. Most of the time
a cow has one calf, but once in a while twins are born.
Like all mammals, cows nurse their babies. Dairy cows
usually nurse their calves for the first few hours.
Then the farmer will feed the calves from a bottle or a bucket.

Only a few weeks old, a horse is learning to run with its mother. Female horses are called mares. Like cows, they usually have one baby at a time. Young horses are called foals until they are a year old.

For several days, a mother hen lays eggs. She sits on them to keep them warm. She may even sit on eggs that are not her own. In three weeks, baby chickens are big enough to hatch. They break out of the eggshells.

Chicks can walk almost as soon as they have hatched. They learn what to eat by watching the hens. Cluck, cluck! A hen is leading some chicks around the yard.

Baby goats are called kids. Only three weeks old, these twins can climb and explore. The female goat is called a nanny.

Searching for food, a goose shows her goslings around the farm. Pigs have big families, too. Piglets always line up in the same order to nurse. The strongest piglet gets the best nipple.

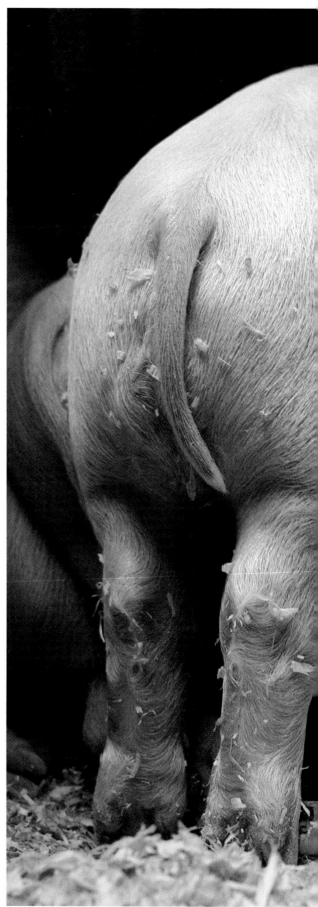

Like children, young farm animals seem to enjoy being together. Piglets often climb on top of each other when they rest. Do you think they are wrestling? By lying close together, they are keeping each other warm.

These baby goats are butting heads. Kids are playful animals. Sometimes their play looks like fighting.

On a farm, where there is open space, it is easy for children to have pets. Animals make good companions. Some children give names to their pets. Lindsay named her fluffy lamb Buttercup.

Baby animals can be fun to cuddle. A soft rabbit and a sleepy piglet both get a hug.

Farm children often learn to ride horses. A farm is a good place for children to enjoy their pets.

At a summer camp, city children have fun while learning how to do farm jobs. These children are giving a mother pig a cool shower on a hot day. The female pig is called a sow.

To stay well, farm animals often need help from people. A farmer carries a new calf to the barn for shelter during a snowstorm.

An animal doctor, or veterinarian, checks a newborn calf to be sure it is healthy. A girl helps another calf find one of its mother's nipples so it can drink the milk right away.

Sometimes animals help farmers do their job. On a ranch, well-trained horses help cowboys round up cattle.
A ranch is a large farm for raising cattle, horses, or sheep.

On some small farms, cows are milked by hand. This farmer treats his thirsty barn cats to a drink of milk.

Cows are milked by machine on most dairy farms. These cows graze in a field until they are ready to be milked.

Then they are taken into the milking parlor. There they are milked by machines with tubes that suck their milk into glass tanks. The milk is then prepared for market. Do you know what foods are made from milk?

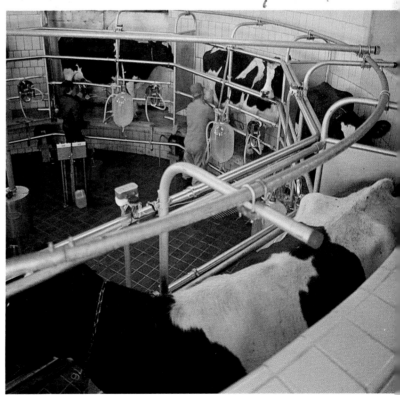

Like milk, most eggs come from special farms. In chicken houses with rows of cages, the hens have food and water all the time.
As the eggs are laid, they roll gently onto a moving shelf to be gathered.

On some family farms, hens lay their eggs in houses called coops. Grandfather shares the chore of collecting eggs by hand.

Another special kind of farm raises turkeys for market. On large farms like this one, the big birds can move around outdoors. The sheds give them shelter from sun and rain.

Many boys and girls join clubs such as 4-H and learn farming skills. Some care for baby farm animals as their special projects. This girl gives her sheep a clipping to groom it for a fair. The children show their animals at the fair to judges, who select the winners. John has won three prizes for his lamb. A happy end to his hard work!

Published by The National Geographic Society
Gilbert M. Grosvenor, *President*
Melvin M. Payne, *Chairman of the Board*
Owen R. Anderson, *Executive Vice President*
Robert L. Breeden, *Vice President, Publications and Educational Media*

Prepared by The Special Publications Division
Donald J. Crump, *Director*
Philip B. Silcott, *Associate Director*
William L. Allen, *Assistant Director*

Staff for this Book
Jane H. Buxton, *Managing Editor*
Jim Abercrombie, *Picture Editor*
Marianne R. Koszorus, *Art Director*
Gail N. Hawkins, *Researcher*
Carol Rocheleau Curtis, *Illustrations Assistant*
Nancy F. Berry, Cricket Brazerol, Dianne T. Craven, Brenda J. Davis, Mary Elizabeth Davis, Rosamund Garner, Cleo Petroff, Sheryl A. Prohovich, Nancy E. Simson, Pamela Black Townsend, Virginia A. Williams, *Staff Assistants*

Engraving, Printing, and Product Manufacture
Robert W. Messer, *Manager*
George V. White, *Production Manager*
George J. Zeller, Jr., *Production Project Manager*
Mark R. Dunlevy, David V. Showers, Gregory Storer, *Assistant Production Managers*
Mary A. Bennett, *Production Assistant;* Julia F. Warner, *Production Staff Assistant*

Consultants
Lynda Ehrlich, *Reading Consultant*
Peter L. Munroe, *Educational Consultant*
Dr. Basil Eastwood, Program Leader, Dairy Production, USDA Extension Service; Dr. Dixon Hubbard, Staff Leader, Livestock and Veterinary Sciences, USDA Extension Service; Stu Sutherland, Public Information Specialist, USDA Extension Service, *Scientific Consultants*

Illustrations Credits
Hans Reinhard/BRUCE COLEMAN INC. (cover, 11, 12 upper, 14); J. C. Carton/BRUCE COLEMAN INC. (1); Julie Habel/WEST LIGHT (2-3, 16 upper, 20); David Overcash/BRUCE COLEMAN INC. (4-5); Grant Heilman/GRANT HEILMAN PHOTOGRAPHY (6 upper left, 6 upper right, 25 lower); David Austin/STOCK BOSTON INC. (6-7); ANIMALS ANIMALS/Margot Conte (8-9); Glenn Eshelman Photography (10-11); Donald Dietz (12 lower); Walter Chandoha (12-13, 32); Charlton Photos (14-15, 30 lower); E. R. Degginger (16 lower); Julie Habel (21 upper, 26 lower, 27); Ed Vidinghoff (17); James H. Karales/PETER ARNOLD INC. (18-19); Tom Myers (21 lower, 30 upper); David Falconer/FOLIO INC. (22-23); Richard Howard/BLACK STAR (24); John Colwell/GRANT HEILMAN PHOTOGRAPHY (25 upper, 26 upper); Audrey Ross/BRUCE COLEMAN INC. (28-29); John Running (31).

Library of Congress CIP Data
Windsor, Merrill, 1924-
    Baby farm animals.

    (Books for young explorers)
    Summary: Describes the characteristics and functions of a variety of domestic animals born and raised on farms.
    1. Domestic animals — Infancy — Juvenile literature. 2. Livestock — Juvenile literature.
[1. Domestic animals. 2. Farm life] I. Title. II. Series.
SF75.5.W55 1984   636'.07   84-16668
ISBN 0-87044-525-1 (regular edition)
ISBN 0-87044-530-8 (library edition)

"Whose barn is this, anyway?"

COVER: Just two days old, twin goats look around curiously at their new world.